When You Finally Said No

poems by

Kathie Giorgio

Finishing Line Press
Georgetown, Kentucky

When You Finally Said No

Copyright © 2019 by Kathie Giorgio
ISBN 978-1-63534-861-3 First Edition
All rights reserved under International and Pan-American Copyright Conventions.
No part of this book may be reproduced in any manner whatsoever without written
permission from the publisher, except in the case of brief quotations embodied in
critical articles and reviews.

Publisher: Leah Maines
Editor: Christen Kincaid
Cover Art: Kathie Giorgio
Author Photo: Ron Wimmer, Wimmer Photography
Cover Design: Leah Huete

Printed in the USA on acid-free paper.
Order online: www.finishinglinepress.com
       also available on amazon.com

              Author inquiries and mail orders:
                    Finishing Line Press
                       P. O. Box 1626
                Georgetown, Kentucky 40324
                         U. S. A.

Table of Contents

My Voice and the Seagull 1

Yellow 3

Heat Is Clean 6

Sexy 7

Rape's in Fashion 9

A Bruised Heart Looks for Love 10

Invisible 11

Under the Sheets 12

Tell the Truth 13

When You Said No 14

Signs 15

Realization 16

Dominoes 18

Living in No's Aftermath 19

Re-Entry 20

Hammock 21

Moonglow 22

Now. Only Me in Here. 23

Today 26

To all of us in this sisterhood that no one would ever choose to join.
There is light.
Breathe.
Live.

#metoo

MY VOICE AND THE SEAGULL

Nine male seagulls
Nine
chase one female over
Chubb Lake.
One.
She dodges
They dive
She ducks
They dive
She screams.

On the deck
I feel her panic
I know the
chaotic heart
propelling limbs
mouth gaped open
breath torn away.
I know it.

Even though I didn't run.
I didn't scream.
Not before.
Not during.

Three.
One.

She, the gull, screams and flies
Before.
I screamed and flew
After.

Nine.
One.
Three.
One.

On the deck
I raise my fists
fling rattled hope into the sky
fight and flight into her feathers
catapult into her soul.

Some would say it's natural,
what's happening to her.
Some would say it's natural,
what happened to me.

She, the gull, bleeds hormones
sending the males into
paroxysms of procreation.
Nine.
One.

I bared denim skin
displayed tight swaying ass
low-buttoned shirt
smiled with my tongue caught
expertly between my teeth
Three.
One.

Years later, on this deck,
I raise my voice
my fists
with her beating wings.

We scream.

YELLOW

I step away and face the woods,
leaving myself behind with my best friend
and the boys she's brought along to this
fire ring.
The boys who delight me.
I think their leers are smiles,
their approaches acceptance,
their touches a choice.
But then they're not and so
I face away.

The woods are verdant with Spring,
the green a green not seen in Winter,
but only in a Wisconsin that is coming
back to life after being frozen and still
for so long.
Behind me, I hear noises and I hold still
but I don't feel green. I feel frozen.

Beneath a tree, there are yellow flowers.
The yellow a new version of the sun.
The petals long and tapered and I want
to run my fingers over them, to see if
they push back.
The way I want to push back.
But I can't.
I'm frozen.

I listen for birds,
I listen for squirrels,
I listen for anything that rustles
or chitters or chirps.
But all I can hear behind me
are guttural laughs

gasps
moans
And a voice I've never heard before.
Even though I know it's mine.

I look at the flowers,
look at the petals,
reach my fingers toward them.
Touch stroke caress,
feel the silk, the smallest bit of sticky,
and I want to fall to my knees,
bury my face in their centers,
breathe
in the pollen

And then it grows quiet.
I stand for a moment more.
Then turn to see myself
lying by the fire ring.
My eyes are closed.
I take note of what's bleeding.
I check to see my chest rise and fall.
I see what's ripped and wonder how
I will ever explain this to my mother
and I fear the punishment.

My best friend is gone.
The boys are moving away. They are
zipping spitting stretching laughing.
They leave me. They leave me there.

When I'm sure they're gone,
I will my eyes to open.
And then I step back inside.

I feel the heat of the yellow
and I sit up to look at the flowers.
And wish I could breathe in the pollen.
Breathe in the scent
The silk
The Spring
But I am now forever in Winter.

HEAT IS CLEAN
　　a list poem

Electric blanket.
Heated seats.
Space heater.
Heating pad.
Hot stone massage.
Tanning bed.
Hot tub.
Hair dryer.
Layers.
Sweaters.
Shower after
shower after
shower.
Years.

When you were thirteen years old
and you ran out of the woods
your clothes were torn
your throat was raw
you were raw.
When you were thirteen years old
you took your first scalding shower
and you've been searing yourself
ever since.
Burning for
sterility. For
purity. For
who you were.
For who you should be.

SEXY

When you try to feel sexy
days after a rape
you reach for a lace chemise
black silk shimmer and soft
And you remember the rip
the pull and the scream
And you stop
set it down.

Gray t-shirt.

When you try to feel sexy
weeks after a rape
you reach for a tight red skirt
slit from your calf to your thigh
And you remember the pull
the scream and the rip
And you stop
set it down.

Gray sweatpants.

When you try to feel sexy
months after a rape
you let your hair fall loose
a tumble of waves on your shoulders
And then you remember the scream
the rip and the pull
And you stop
pull it into a ponytail.

Cut it off at your scalp.

When you try to feel sexy
years after a rape
you reach for your favorite red lipstick
draw it over the curved pout of your mouth
And then you remember the scream
the scream and the scream
And you stop
wipe it all blank with a tissue.

Bare-faced.

When you sit at your mirror
forever after a rape
you are not your reflection.
You remember it all, what
came after the scream.
And you stop.
Lock the door.
Close your eyes.

There will be no sexy today.

RAPE'S IN FASHION
a haiku

sideboob   cameltoe
ass cleavage   fuck-me boots
we molest with style

A BRUISED HEART LOOKS FOR LOVE
a villanelle with a slant

Only some women can understand
a bruised heart red with hope.
She will learn to trust this man.

In bed, his force was fierce and strong,
swollen desire gone past the bounds.
Only some women can understand.

Kiss-soaked afterglow, a whispered word,
her body reflected her heart.
She will want to trust this man.

His voice a balm, the hurt a hum,
until it all began again.
Only some women can understand.

Pain and love go hand in hand.
Red raised to heat, her heart is full.
Only some women can understand.
She will always trust this man.

INVISIBLE

You say nothing.
In fear of his yes. In fear of your no.
Both words are magical.
Poof! You disappear.

UNDER THE SHEETS

When I am with you under the sheets
shiver meets sizzle and sweat
and heat always rises to the top.
Fingers brush thighs and tongues lap tips
and breaths blend in mists of icefire.

When I am with you under the sheets
love meets blue and black
and red always rises to the top.
Nothing is soft and you're fierce and I'm weak
and wretched with your demands of desire.

When I am with you under the sheets
love meets smack and slap
and loss always rises to the top.
The mattress sinks low and I am sold
as property you can acquire.

But when I'm alone and throw back the sheets
the moon kills the black of the sky
and silver always rises to the top.
It bleaches my skin and I glow on my own
but always sink back in your mire.

TELL THE TRUTH
a villanelle

Sometimes your love feels just like fear;
the trembles, the gasps and the cries.
This is the truth you don't want to hear.

You just can't breathe when he is near,
his mouth steals your voice with his sighs.
Sometimes your love feels just like fear.

His voice so soft within your ear,
but his words that softness denies.
This is the truth you don't want to hear.

But he's the one you hold most dear.
With him, you don't dare speak lies.
Sometimes your love feels just like fear.

What he wants is never clear.
He calls, you come, you die.
This is the truth you don't want to hear.

This will go on year after year.
Your soul, entrapped, won't fly.
Sometimes your love feels just like fear.
This is the truth you don't want to hear.

WHEN YOU SAID NO
> *NO: adverb*
> *a negative used to express dissent, denial, or refusal,*
> *as in response to a question, request or demand*

when you said no
and he said nothing
the earth spun dizzy beneath your feet
the sky above, blue as columbine, became the black of your clenched eyes
the birdsong raucous with the shrieks you swallowed
the grass tender beneath you like nails into your skin
and he, the potential, the prince, the man who held the door, who held
your coat, who held your hand, who said your name and your identifying
consonants and vowels were like peppermint on his tongue
and yes, you wanted that tongue
sweet in your mouth
the way he said your name sweet in your mouth
his hand a gentleman's glove on your breast
you said yes you said yes
but then the glove was off
bared the knuckles beneath

when you said no
and he said nothing
and the world twisted off kilter
blueblack sky
birdvoice screamsongs
grass of nails
his tongue no longer sweet and no longer saying your name
but transforming you from princess to slut

when you said no
and he said nothing
he walked away, his hands in the pockets of his grass-stained jeans,
whistling to the next date in line, already set for Saturday
and you learned to say nothing as well

SIGNS

a prose poem

and when he is over you and blocks out all light   there is nothing to do but go inside   but instead of hiding in the shadows of your heart   you find yourself at the entrance to your brain   a white-tissued labyrinth that twines straight ahead   a place where you won't get lost   a place where there are no choices   other than move ahead or go back   and so you move ahead and as you do the sounds around you   the thumpbumpbangs   the vibrations that are wracking your ribs cracking your teeth snapping your hips   fade   fade into barely there   like a thought that you can't quite remember   what is happening to you now   you move through the white tissue   turn left turn right   and always go further in   in and in but not down   and the light does not change   until it does   you step out onto a bright green lawn   a whitewalled room   not big not small   just large enough for a bench and a glance   you sit   the sounds are gone   there is light and air and green   and signs, you notice   white signs all stuck on posts into the grass   four of them   all facing you   one says NO   one says STOP   the third says This is MY body   and the fourth says You may not You may not You WILL not   you read them   one by one   and then you read them in reverse You WILL not You may not You may not   This is MY body   STOP   NO   the thought that you can't grasp goes deeper   you feel it there in your bones   in the shadow of your heart   in the pit of your stomach   in that fragile place of entry   and when you stand   you feel the ache   you don't want to remember   you stoop for a minute   back bent knees bent   and there's no choice but to go ahead or go back   you straighten   it hurts but you straighten   you pluck the signs like flowers   a rose a tulip a lily a sunflower   and then you rest them on your shoulder like a picket   like a protest   and like a protest you begin   a steady march out   and when you return to the dark   to the beneath   to the buried   to the blocked air blocked light blocked life   when you return to your bed   you brandish the signs like weapons   you pull up your knee like a weapon   you plant each sign at each of the four corners of your bed   facing out   and you shout   No. You say no, you say. No. You say no.

REALIZATION

> *"No woman should be shamefaced in attempting to give back to the world, through her work, a portion of its lost heart."*   —Louise Bogan

I can say yes to the first boy who begs me.
And I can say yes to the first man I beg.
I can say yes to whomever I want.
And I can say no to you.
My past does not say yes.
My present does not say yes.
My future does not say yes.
I do.
And I can say no to you.

I can say yes to CraigsList trysts.
And I can say yes to meetups in bars.
I can say yes to 800-sexts.
And I can say no to you.
My actions do not say yes.
My mistakes do not say yes.
My impulses do not say yes.
I do.
And I can say no to you.

I can say yes to this sheer blouse.
And I can say yes to this slit skirt.
I can say yes to these fuck-me boots.
And I can say no to you.
My curves do not say yes.
My cleavage does not say yes.
My bare thighs do not say yes.
I do.
And I can say no to you.

I can scream yes to you through the night.
And I can sigh yes to you in the morning.
I can shout yes to you all weekend long.
And I can say no to you too.
I can moan yes to you in my bed.
And I can plead yes bent over my table.
I can cry yes to you on the floor.
And I can say no to you too.
Positions do not say yes.
Time after time does not say yes.
Our history does not say yes.
I do.
And I can say no to you too.

DOMINOES

I love you more than I've ever loved anyone,
he says, and then he looks over her shoulder,
winks at another woman and walks away.
She waits in his echo for months,
joining others who stand in a long line
facing west.
And then like dominoes,
they fall.

LIVING IN NO'S AFTERMATH
a villanelle

With you, I was crazy; without you, I'm insane.
Then, I filled your desire. Now, I've ceased to exist.
I have been wholly consumed by your flame.

There was a time when I wasn't ashamed;
when your body absorbed mine, when I embodied your kiss.
With you, I was crazy; without you, I'm insane.

I know I have just myself to blame.
Sucked in by your words, your eyes, your fist.
I have been wholly consumed by your flame.

Without you, I'm lost, but with you, I'm maimed.
Yet there is so much of you and me that I miss.
With you, I was crazy; without you, I'm insane.

With you, I felt that Love could be named.
But you are a lie, your promise a twist.
I have been wholly consumed by your flame.

Enraptured by you, one of Satan's men,
your seraphim heat, I just couldn't resist.
 With you, I was crazy; without you, I'm insane.
I have been wholly consumed by your flame.

RE-ENTRY
    a haiku

This body, my own.
Treasure trove to be opened
by whom I choose.

HAMMOCK

I rest in the hammock of the crescent moon
and dream of nights that were full
when I raised my hands to the corduroy sky
and cupped the moon in my palms.
I breathed empty space and falling stars
gossamer light and audacious black.
I dream. The way it used to be.
Full.
Now, I rest in all that's left
set the hammock moon to swinging
and sway to the other side.

MOONGLOW
haiku

my eyes see the moon
but it's my soul that glows bright
silver reflection.

NOW. ONLY ME IN HERE.

Why is it lately when
I'm giving head, I'm
thinking of poetry
not porn?
Used to be I thought of porn
all the time while doing this
and other things. Many things.
All things.
I thought of how I'd look on that
screen or that stage or straddled on
that set of hips and it would
make me do what I was doing
faster. Better for the one I was
with, for sure.
And me too, being there, and
living the double life in my mind.

But now, in my fifties, instead of
15, 18, 20, 30, 40, 43,
oh, 43, the wonder of that year,
just over a decade ago and how
long ago a decade seems,
but now, I think of this tired body
and I wince.
No screen anymore, except for
yearly mammograms and I do
have to make that appointment
for the up the butt colonoscopy.
Which is something I've never enjoyed
and isn't it good I'm finally saying no.

I never said no.
I should have said no.
I wanted to.

So I don't think of porn.
I think of poetry.

I still get out, I still meet with men,
and over dinner, over drinks, over
coffee, over his held hands, I flirt.
But I know, even as I do, even as
I run my tongue over my lips, lower
my voice, lean forward for his glimpse
of my cleavage, my heart's just not
in it anymore.

It just seems like so much work.

At hotels, I do what's expected, what
I promised without thinking, but
I can't help but think
I'd rather be in the hot tub than a hot
bed. I'd rather be in the embrace
of a blanket, sunk in the sweetness
of sleep, the sweetness of dreams
and solitude, than in the sweetness
of sex. Of afterglow. That glow is
dimmed.

Really, the only one I want to romance
is myself.
The only one I want to seduce
is myself.
But even that seduction involves
blankets and warm drinks and cozy
chairs and great books.
No fingers. No toys.
More pleasure
than self-pleasing.

So who the hell am I now?
I'm not used to being so dry, so
totally unmoved by a man, by
Possibilities.
Maybe this is the new part of my life.
The new blending into the old.
No more monthly blood.
No more yearning for a touch between
the legs, behind the ear lobe, on the tip
of a nipple, or lips on my neck.
But yearning for quiet.

I no longer glow with the heat
of my hormones, but the heat of my
thoughts. And memory.
Maybe the tick of the clock I hear
isn't the clock at all, but the beat of
my own heart.
No longer a biological clock.
A lifetime clock.
Running down.

TODAY

Waking up
in my own company
with only my skin
my warmth
my bones
my mind
(just me!)
brings new meaning
to a new day.

KATHIE GIORGIO is the critically acclaimed author of four novels, *The Home For Wayward Clocks* (2011), *Learning To Tell (A Life)Time* (2013), *Rise From The River* (2015), and *In Grace's Time* (2017), two story collections, *Enlarged Hearts* (2012) and *Oddities & Endings; The Collected Stories Of Kathie Giorgio* (2016), a collection of essays, *Today's Moment Of Happiness Despite The News; A Year Of Spontaneous Essays* (2018), and two poetry chapbooks, *True Light Falls In Many Forms* (2016) and *When You Finally Said No* (2019). Giorgio's short stories and poems have appeared in countless literary magazines and anthologies. Her short story, *Snapdragon*, was performed on stage for the Stories On Stage series at Su Teatro theatre in Boulder, Colorado. She's been nominated for the Pushcart Prize, the Write Well Award, the Million Writer Award, and for the Best of the Net Anthology. Her novel *The Home For Wayward Clocks* won the 2011 Outstanding Achievement Award from the Wisconsin Library Association. Her novel *In Grace's Time* was runner-up in fiction in the 2017 Maxy Award and the second place winner of the 2017 Silver Pen Award For Literary Excellence. Giorgio is the director/founder of AllWriters' Workplace & Workshop. She lives in Waukesha, Wisconsin, with her husband, mystery writer Michael Giorgio, her 18-year old daughter Olivia, who is writing her first novel, a neurotic dog named after Ursula LeGuin, a fat cat named Edgar Allen Paw, and a tiny cat named Muse.

www.ingramcontent.com/pod-product-compliance
Lightning Source LLC
LaVergne TN
LVHW041518070426
835507LV00012B/1662